The Drumbeat
of Life

The Drumbeat of Life

JUBILEE IN AN AFRICAN CONTEXT

SEBASTIAN BAKARE

WCC Publications, Geneva

Cover design: Chaz Maviyane-Davies

IBSN 2-8254-1229-5

© 1997 WCC Publications, World Council of Churches,
150 route de Ferney, 1211 Geneva 2, Switzerland

No. 80 in the Risk Book Series

Printed in Switzerland

Table of Contents

vii   INTRODUCTION

1   1. THE DRUMBEAT OF LIFE

12   2. AFRICA'S GROWING CHURCHES

20   3. JUBILEE AND AFRICAN REALITIES

39   4. THE ECUMENICAL FUTURE AND THE CHURCHES OF AFRICA

Introduction

The general public in Zimbabwe knows very little about the World Council of Churches, its functions and activities. Many of those who are acquainted with it are persons who were outside the country during the war of liberation and who came to know the Council chiefly for its support in the struggle against the unjust colonial settler regime. The regime for its part regarded the WCC, especially the Programme to Combat Racism, as an extension of international communism. Consequently, any positive accounts of the Council and its work were censored.

The coming of the WCC's eighth assembly to Zimbabwe in 1998 is therefore of great significance, since it offers Zimbabwean Christians a first-hand opportunity to get to know the work of the organization and its vocation. Many will be privileged to interact with delegates and other participants and to hear stories, not only of the WCC and its activities, but also of the life of the Christian churches which make it up.

In this short book about the theme of the eighth assembly, "Turn to God – Rejoice in Hope", I have attempted to highlight some of the issues I consider vital from my own perspective as a Zimbabwean Christian who has grown to cherish the work of the WCC ever since my first encounter at its fourth assembly in Uppsala, Sweden, in 1968. At that time the assembly was challenged by delegates from the third world who were concerned about what they saw as paternalism by the North towards the so-called "younger churches". Thirty years have since gone by, and the WCC as an instrument of the ecumenical movement finds itself faced with new challenges and opportunities. When the WCC assembly met in Nairobi in 1975, there were still countries in Africa, including Zimbabwe, that were under colonial regimes. Today the continent is completely free from foreign colonial rule, but it is faced with a range of new and difficult challenges.

WCC assemblies have always created a forum not only for fellowship among Christians but also for solidarity with those in need. We must hope and pray that the spirit of togetherness and willingness to hear the cries of a broken world will also be dominant in the deliberations of the eighth assembly. The church of God is called to be a herald of the message of repentance, as the assembly theme suggests. *Turning to God* is not possible without repentance. The church is called to lead the world to God. In Africa, despite the astonishing numerical growth of the church, Christians are only too aware of the social evils which are destroying human life. Corruption, political mismanagement and economic exploitation by both local elites and external multinationals remain a major concern for the poor majority on the continent.

At the same time there is also reason to *rejoice in hope* over the more positive developments Africa is experiencing, especially in the area of political democratization. There have also been achievements in education, health and other social amenities which were denied to the majority of the people during the colonial era. As a result of some of these developments, women, considered in traditional Zimbabwean society, for example, as minors, are increasingly taking their rightful place in society. This has been facilitated by new laws which have removed discriminatory practices in areas such as inheritance, land ownership, educational opportunities and employment. A growing number of women are taking leadership positions in government, industry and commerce. At the same time, it is women who are spearheading development in rural areas.

* * *

I would like to acknowledge the support I have received from my friend John Pobee, who sharpened some of my unclear thoughts about the structures of the WCC. Thanks also go to my wife Ruth, who has maintained a keen interest in the WCC since her first encounter with it at the Ecumenical Institute of Bossey in the mid-1960s and then as a steward in Uppsala (1968). She has assisted me in putting the text on the computer – with great diligence and patience.

Finally, I would like to thank the WCC for according me this opportunity to popularize the theme of the assembly from an African perspective.

1. The Drumbeat of Life

To an African, the theme of the forthcoming eighth assembly of the World Council of Churches, "Turn to God – Rejoice in Hope", evokes the image of those moments when members of the community are invited to gather at the centre of the village and join the circle of dancers. Accompanied by the sound of the drumbeat, *Pangu-Pangu-Pangu*, such an invitation can be heard far and near.

One of the precious gifts God has given to Africans is the gift of singing and dancing. Africans dance on all sorts of occasions to express their inner feelings, whether of joy or of sorrow. While the dancing is spontaneous and voluntary, the drumbeat provides the rhythm that holds the dancers together.

As the drumbeat sounds, *Pangu-Pangu-Pangu*, the leader chants the invitation to gather together in rhythmic words. A song from the Ewe people is typical (although the English translation cannot convey the rhythm of the original):

All of you, all of you,
Come-come-come-come,
Let us dance
In the evening
When the sky has gone down the river.

Down the ground
Come-come-come-come,
Strengthen yourselves.

We don't want meetings
With mats and beds.
We want a gathering of dancing.
Men, women and children,
We have all gone,
We left long ago,
Mats and beds remain behind.

Although drums in more recent years have become ornaments for decorating the home as well as popular souvenirs for tourists to Zimbabwe and other African countries, their primary function remains their role in cultural activities and rituals. In villages throughout the continent, the sound and rhythm of the drum express the mood of the people. The drum is a sign of life; its beat is the heartbeat of the community.

Such is the power of the drum to evoke emotions, to touch the souls of those who hear its rhythms, that the earliest Christian missionaries to Africa forbade its use in church services, imposing instead the organ or piano, "sober" instruments whose appeal was meant to be cerebral rather than emotional.

A poem by T. Viki, published in the *Mambo Book of Zimbabwean Verse* (1986), captures well the way in which the sound of the drumbeat and of singing keeps people together in Africa. She writes:

Africa, you are symbolized
By the beating of the drums
The drumbeat everywhere
Please don't drift away.

We are joyful nature's musicians,
We need not be taught to sing,
Our voices, tongues and lips are blessed.
Please don't drift away.

Africa, you have many sounds.
Sounds in the morning,
At noon, at night.
Sounds of women humming,
When grinding maize,
Singing at the well,
And when babies cry,
Or go to sleep on their mothers' back.
Please don't drift away.

Africa's men sing when they hunt,
They sing when one has died.
Please don't drift away.

The drums of Harare

When participants from churches around the world gather in Harare for the WCC's eighth assembly in December 1998, this sound of the drum will play a similar role in calling members of churches from every continent to assemble and celebrate God's gift of life. This sound will set their mood;

the rhythmic beat of the drum will symbolize the desire expressed in the ecumenical movement to drift together, like an African village community, under the transforming power of the Holy Spirit.

To be sure, the experience of the ecumenical movement over the 50 years since the first assembly of the World Council of Churches in 1948 has shown that when you drift together there are bound to be some who lag behind, some who question the speed and the direction of the movement to which all are being invited, even some who turn a deaf ear to the rhythm of the drum. These individual drifters, like individualistic dancers, pose a challenge to the community. To them comes the call, "Please don't drift away."

In an African community, coming together in response to the beating of the drum is an opportunity to give one another a sense of belonging and of solidarity. It is a time to connect with each other, to be part of that collective rhythm of life in which young and old, rich and poor, men and women are all invited to contribute the gifts God has given them. As they celebrate life and offer these gifts, they in turn receive new energies, new orientations and security.

For the African, dancing is thus therapeutic. This does not mean that you "dance away your problems"; rather, you dance *with* them in the rhythm of life which includes both sorrow and happiness. In a continent well known for its ability to endure suffering, the appeal in the WCC assembly theme to "turn to God" resonates with everyday experience. For Africans, turning to God is a completely normal thing; indeed, life would be unimaginable if we did not have the possibility of turning to God for protection and help. Africans expect God to be with them, to see them through droughts and wars and diseases, through exploitation and oppression and slavery, through all of life and through death. Africans naturally turn to the God who participates in their suffering. A common expression used during times of crisis by the Shona-speaking people of Zimbabwe is "*Mwari ega ndiye anoziva*" – "only God knows our plight". Life would be unthinkable without this dependence on God.

So, too, when delegates from the WCC's member churches around the world gather in Harare and hear the drumbeat calling them to join together in a community to strengthen each other and receive strength, they will witness to their own dependence on God. They will tell stories from their own contexts of turning to God; they will share their testimonies of experiences with the God who alone knows their plight, the God whose faithfulness has been shown again and again.

At the same time, the other appeal in the assembly theme, the call to "rejoice in hope", will set the mood for the assembly in Harare. The drumbeat will be inviting people together for a celebration. While joyful celebration has been an element of each of the Council's previous assemblies, it will be especially resonant in Harare because the eighth assembly comes during the year of the 50th anniversary of the founding of the WCC. A special ceremony of grateful remembrance of the past fifty years and solemn recommitment for the coming new millennium is planned for the end of the assembly. Throughout the 12 days of the assembly, in formal remarks in public sessions, in hymns and responses during worship services and in private conversations during encounters over coffee or around the table at mealtime, those who have been present at previous WCC assemblies, including some who were there in Amsterdam in 1948 when the Council was born, will share stories about the remarkable steps towards unity taken by Christians and churches – through God's grace and under the leading of the Holy Spirit – during these past 50 years.

The WCC's recent policy statement "Towards a Common Understanding and Vision of the World Council of Churches" summarizes some of the "signs of obedience and faithfulness" that the churches in the WCC have been empowered by God's grace to set up during this half-century:
– building and maintaining fragile links of communication when they have found themselves on opposite sides of wars, hot and cold;

– offering service in the name of Christ to millions driven from their homes, and helping to rebuild societies shattered by violence, thus learning new forms of mutual sharing;
– challenging each other to let go of historic bonds of dependence and dominance, and forging new kinds of partnership;
– offering common witness to Jesus Christ in places where a single voice would not have been heard or taken seriously;
– listening to and learning from the insights of others into those central understandings of doctrine and life over which they are divided, persisting stubbornly in the hope of seeing the day when unity in one faith and one eucharistic fellowship will be made visible;
– offering pastoral support in many places where human dignity has been trampled, and joining their voices with others to defend in international forums the rights of those oppressed and pushed to the edges;
– expressing solidarity in prayer and encouragement with those churches suffering persecution or seeking God's will amidst situations of crisis;
– refusing to turn away from the judgment that every form of racism, also in their own life, is contrary to the word and will of God;
– committing themselves to solidarity with women, challenging structures that reinforce sexism and insisting on justice and full participation for women in church and world;
– seeking to make their own communities and the instruments of their fellowship together more fully inclusive of women, youth, persons with disabilities and all others threatened with exclusion;
– joining in intercessions and prayers using each other's words and music, and learning how to read the scripture through each other's eyes.

African Christians will recognize with gratitude many of these signs of hope. What will especially come to mind for many Christians in the southern part of the continent, including Zimbabwe, is the solidarity of the churches around the world in the struggle against racism and the courageous and costly support for our liberation through the Council's Programme to Combat Racism.

I remember well the almost deliriously joyful crowd that gathered on 18 April 1980 in Rufaro Stadium in Harare – the planned venue for one of the major celebrations of the eighth assembly – to celebrate the birth of the new nation of Zimbabwe, finally freed from colonial rule and domination by the white minority after a liberation struggle of many years. The masses of people sang and danced. Some cried for joy; others wept for dear ones who had lost their lives in the struggle or were unable for other reasons to experience the joyful birth of the nation. Rhythmic drumbeats and clapping and flashes of colourful flags made the occasion an unforgettable one for all who were present or watched the celebration on television.

For Christians the supreme occasion for celebration is of course the resurrection of Jesus Christ. They cannot bear witness to the good news of his resurrection without celebration. "Alleluia, Christ is Risen!" "He is risen indeed!" is a familiar liturgical form of greeting in many Christian traditions during the Easter season. Christian life, as a witness to the resurrection and the redemption it has brought, is a life of celebration.

The biblical jubilee
The WCC's eighth assembly is being described as a "jubilee assembly". The word "jubilee" is of course often used to refer to any significant anniversary, especially a 50th anniversary. But behind the origins of the English word "jubilee" lies an important biblical tradition, which is given its most explicit definition in the law code recorded in Leviticus 25.

According to this tradition, every 50th year was to be a year of jubilee. Celebrations were to be held for the whole year. Land and animals were to rest, debts were to be cancelled, land was to be returned to its original owners. The jubilee year was, in short, a year of grace. In the book of Isaiah, the prophet picks up this theme in the expression "the year of the Lord's favour" (Isa. 61:2).

Characteristic of this year of the Lord's favour was the spirit of forgiveness. Jubilee was meant to be a time to renew broken human relationships with each other and with God, a time to share the messianic hope, a time to comfort those who were mourning (cf. Isa. 40). The spirit of jubilee was also one of rededication to the needs of the poor and of those who found themselves on the losing side of unjust human arrangements – such as the laws which deprived debtors of their land and thus their livelihood, in effect reducing them to slavery. The jubilee was furthermore a time of reconciliation. Victimizer and victim were called to repent and forgive, to treat one another as equals, to give each other the opportunity to start life anew without victimization.

The fact that the jubilee year was inaugurated on the Day of Atonement underscored God's demand for purity of heart as a necessary condition for any true reconciliation. In the context of ancient Israel, this year of liberty, rejoicing and reconciliation was to be proclaimed not by the sound of the drumbeat as in Africa, but by the sounding of the *yobel*, the Hebrew word for the ram's horn (from which the word "jubilee" is derived).

The prescriptions for the jubilee year clearly reflect the context of an agrarian society controlled by unjust land laws which sanctioned the dispossession of poor peasant farmers from their land. Threatened with slavery for their entire family if they were unable to pay their debts, these victims of the prevailing social and economic order would surely have greeted with jubilation the jubilee year and the prospect of redemption and being reunited with their families, for this would signal a new beginning, a fresh start on the basis of equality. The slaveholders and land-grabbers would be reminded that God does not approve of slavery but wants freedom for all God's people. One can imagine, then, that those in power would not particularly have welcomed the coming of the jubilee year.

8

Although there is no evidence in the Bible or other ancient sources that the jubilee as prescribed in Leviticus 25 was ever actually put into practice, the ideas behind it were clearly picked up, not only in the prophecy of Isaiah, as we saw above, but also by Jesus when he announced to the synagogue in Nazareth the missionary programme that would mark the new messianic era to be fulfilled in his person:

> The Spirit of the Lord is upon me,
> because he has anointed me
> to bring good news to the poor.
> He has sent me to proclaim release to the captives
> and recovery of sight to the blind,
> to let the oppressed go free,
> to proclaim the year of the Lord's favour (Luke 4:18-19).

Jesus proclaims the good news to the poor who are victims of an unjust society. This good news is indeed bad news to the rich and powerful, who will be sent away empty (Luke 1:53). Jesus sees himself as the fulfilment of the messianic hope announced in the passage from the prophecy of Isaiah which he read in the synagogue. During the jubilee, the year of the Lord's favour, the time of fulfilment of the messianic hope, all are to experience a change in their lives.

When old Simeon in the temple saw the baby Jesus, he witnessed the fulfilment of God's promise to his people Israel. His wish is to die joyfully, because he has witnessed and experienced the long-awaited promise:

> Master, now you are dismissing your servant in peace,
> according to your word;
> for my eyes have seen your salvation,
> which you have prepared in the presence of all peoples,
> a light for revelation to the Gentiles
> and for glory to your people Israel (Luke 2:29-30).

Similarly, the jubilee is an eschatological foretaste of a heavenly life, full of peace, justice, equality, love – of everything that makes life more purposeful and worth living.

Certainly in Zimbabwe – and I suspect elsewhere – the biblical jubilee is a virtually unknown theme. The text from

Luke 4 which records Jesus' inaugural sermon is often used as a basis for sermons on Christian responsibility towards oppressed people, but nine of ten preachers whom I recently interviewed in Harare who had preached on the Luke 4 text said they had not done so in the context of its biblical antecedents in the jubilee. Thus for the eighth assembly, we need to find a common language that expresses the spirit of jubilee.

The celebration of the jubilee is not an occasion for triumphalism. Rather, we are called to be humble before God who is the host of the jubilee celebration. As we see Christians from around the world moving together in response to the drumbeat at the assembly, symbolizing their aspirations to move closer to one another in the ecumenical movement, we cannot ignore other types of movement in our world today. For example, we are reminded of the mobility of jobs and capital which characterizes contemporary capitalism, to the advantage of a few, while in Zimbabwe, as in many other countries, it is creating another kind of movement: the migration of rural poor people to urban centres in an often fruitless search for work. The development of shanty towns on the peripheries of our urban centres attests to this undermining of the basic rural economy. In Zimbabwe and other poor countries, the servicing of the central debt which has been incurred as a result of this international financial system is leeching away resources that might otherwise have gone into growth, moving the profits to already rich countries in the North. Our understanding of the biblical jubilee, also during this jubilee assembly, must be linked to such realities, in the recognition that this jubilee vision is not a human social and economic system devised by benevolent do-gooders, but a vision of God's plan for sharing the resources with which he has endowed the human family.

How do we propose to share God's gifts at the jubilee assembly? Each person present will express the biblical meaning of jubilee in his or her own way. The celebration of the jubilee will also be an occasion to relate our life stories to those of others through common worship, in fellowship created by biblical reflections, meditation and music. In worshipping together we shall listen to God's "still, small voice" pointing us to the direction the ecumenical movement and the churches must take. Sadly, this worship cannot yet include a complete sharing of the eucharist. "Turn to God – Rejoice in Hope" is thus also a call to repent from our inability to overcome that which makes us unready to accept Jesus as the host of the eucharist. It is only the repentant sinner who has access to the kingdom of God (cf. Matt. 3:2; 4:17; Luke 15).

The God who turns to us through the Son wants us to establish new relationships based on love with each other and with God. In this relationship love of self disappears and love of neighbour grips our life. This love of neighbour remains elusive, and it is our task and challenge to make it possible as we celebrate our jubilee. God wants us to come home, and to feel at home in each other's company. As it was for the Prodigal Son in Jesus' story, home for us is a place we may choose to get away from so long as we are gripped by an unrepentant mood. Disobedience becomes our master when we turn away from God's love and mercy, when we refuse to heed the call of the prophet Micah "to do justice, and to love kindness, and to walk humbly with our God" (6:8). Jubilee invites us to act justly and to enter into a new relationship with God and with each other.

The assembly will provide an opportunity to relive the memories of our human brokenness due to sins of racial and gender discrimination, social and economic exploitation, political oppression and the many other social evils committed by individuals or groups of people or systems. Where we do not act in love, we sin, and sin dehumanizes us and destroys our integrity.

In traditional African community human relations are of greater value than gold and silver. Good relationships enjoyed by members of the community create a sense of hope and security in a world that breeds hostility and hopelessness, where morality has broken down and there seem to be no rules to guide human behaviour. Where we have lost these values, we have also lost our fundamental relationship with God the Creator. We need to name the sins which create rifts among us and between ourselves and God which make it impossible for us to move together along the way to unity.

The context in which we are called to proclaim the freedom and forgiveness and reconciliation of the jubilee is one of division and divisiveness – between black and white, rich and poor, North and South, "developed" and "underdeveloped". Amidst such divisions, what legitimacy and credibility for announcing the good news can a divided church have? The secular world does not apologize for drawing lines and creating divisions and building blocs, because it does not claim what the church proclaims: the unity of the members of the body of Christ. Ecumenism is thus not something optional but an imperative. Unity is what Jesus wills. The jubilee assembly is thus an opportunity to ask God's forgiveness for considering church unity a mere option rather than a requirement of our faith.

What might the jubilee mean in the context of the world and the church today, as the churches prepare specifically to come to Africa and to listen to the drumbeats calling them to the eighth assembly of the World Council of Churches? As the delegates of the churches come to this continent, they come to a region of the world where Christianity is experiencing phenomenal growth – an exciting (though also, as we shall see, challenging) reality. They also come to a continent which is largely – and perhaps for too many people exclusively – known as a place of hunger, disease, poverty, exploitation, political instability and misery.

We shall look at some facets of both of these African realities in the following chapters, as we try to discern some of the dimensions of this movement which the drums of Harare will again call together in December 1998.

2. Africa's Growing Churches

When the delegates gathered in Amsterdam in 1948 for the WCC's first assembly, the number of persons from Africa among them was very small, and a good number of those were in fact Europeans and North Americans representing Western mission agencies working in Africa. Fifty years ago, most African countries were colonies of European powers, and the churches there were outposts of mission agencies from Europe and North America. As successive WCC assemblies have welcomed an increasing number of member churches from all over the world, there has also been a growing presence of Africans representing their own churches. "Turn to God – Rejoice in Hope" is thus an invitation to celebrate this evidence of God's faithfulness as well.

In fact, this jubilee assembly will take place at a time when the Christian church in Africa is witnessing phenomenal and vibrant growth. Along with what is happening elsewhere in the southern hemisphere, this growth has led many observers to say that the "centre of gravity" of the church worldwide has shifted away from Europe and North America.

Despite material deprivation and poverty, despite social and economic marginalization, despite persecution and pressures from other religions, Christianity is growing faster in Africa than anywhere else in the world. While this dynamic numerical growth is indeed a source of joy for the entire ecumenical movement, it should not tempt African churches themselves to become complacent or to ignore the challenges facing them. The moment of grace signalled by this demographic shift in the world church calls Christians in Africa to creative imagination and new vision in their mission.

The African worldview

It is not possible to understand the church in Africa without some acquaintance with the anthropology and worldview which are part and parcel of African religion. Within the short space available in this book, it is of course impossible to give a complete account of this, and the brief remarks here draw heavily on the part of Africa from which I come.

The Shona people have a profound belief in *Mwari*, God the creator who sustains and is in control of the world. Nothing that human beings do escapes his notice. It is important to understand that this world which *Mwari* sustains is the world of the living and the world of the "timeless living" (the deceased). Life does not end with physical death; it continues to remain under *Mwari*'s control, but at a higher level. People do not die, but pass on from this world to the next, the world of spirits.

But admission into this world of spirits is not automatic, as G. Chavunduka notes in *Traditional Medicine in Modern Zimbabwe*. One must be accepted and admitted into it. During a special ritual, the relatives who remain behind must hand over the spirit of the deceased to the other ancestral spirits.

The Shona consider *Mwari*, the Great Spirit, the unapproachable supreme being, as being interested not in the affairs of individuals but of communities. Human beings can communicate with him only through intermediaries. The following prayer, cited by E.W. Smith in *African Ideas of God*, illustrates symbolically some of the elements of the Shona conception of *Mwari*:

> *Great Spirit!*
> *Piler up of the rock into towering mountains!*
> *When you stamp on the stone,*
> *The dust rises and fills the land.*
> *Hardness of the precipice;*
> *Waters of the pool that turn*
> *Into misty rain when stirred.*
> *Vessel overflowing with oil:*
> *Father of Runji,*
> *Who sews heavens like cloth:*
> *Let him knit together that which is below.*
> *Caller of the branching trees:*
> *You bring forth the shoots*
> *That they stand erect.*
> *You have filled the land with humankind,*
> *the dust rises on high, O Lord!*
> *Wonderful one, you live*

In the midst of rain to humankind:
We pray to you,
Hear us, Lord!
Show mercy when we beseech you, Lord.
You are òn high with the spirits of the great.
You raise the grass-covered hills
Above the earth, and create the rivers,
Gracious one.

The Shona idea of God must be seen in the context of African anthropology, which in turn cannot be understood apart from the concept of community. The community defines the way of life for its members and gives the individual a sense of belonging to an extended family, tribe or clan. A good African is one who cherishes values of community life. This African understanding of community does not divide reality into "secular" and "religious"; it is all one community. Everything revolves around it; and outside the community is mere emptiness. God is the source of life, and the community draws its existence from God.

In this understanding of community, human beings, the living and the living dead, are linked in a chain of communication with each other and with God. This communication may take place through dreams, visions or trances. Dreams are thus to be taken seriously as a means of communication with ancestors who are already living in a spiritual world. These ancestors are believed to cause dreams in order to communicate with still-living offspring. African Christian theologian John Mbiti explains that

> the importance of dreams in African Christian experience can be appreciated when viewed against the traditional background in which the visible and the invisible worlds interlock at main points. The attitude that dreams have a supernatural significance falls within the normal view that many ordinary experiences are often regarded or seen to have a mystical or supernatural dimension to them. Dreams will therefore bridge these two worlds.

Since the message of a dream is not always as immediately evident to a person as was the dream of Joseph recorded in

Genesis 37, many people who have had a dream will visit a traditional healer for interpretation. The healer will then go into a trance in order to consult with those who have caused the dream in order to be able to convey the message to the person.

One area in which dreams have an important role is the practice of traditional medicine. A traditional healer does not simply go into the bush to look for herbs from any tree, but is directed in a dream by his or her ancestors to a specific tree whose herbs can provide the right substance to heal the particular disease.

Western-oriented and African independent churches

There are two major types of Christian churches found in all parts of Africa. Each of these types is known by several different names and none of these names seems to be entirely satisfactory to everyone. On the one hand are the churches which were founded by Western missionary agencies and which are often referred to as mainline or historic churches; most of the African member churches of the WCC fall into this category. On the other hand are churches established by Africans which make a much more concerted effort to take seriously the African worldview and its religious thought-forms. These latter churches are called African independent churches (the term we shall use in this book) or sometimes African-instituted churches or African initiatives in Christianity. Only a few of these churches are members of the WCC, although contacts between them and the Council have been increasing in recent years.

The Western-oriented Christian churches of Africa tend to have the same ecclesiastical structures and doctrines as their mother churches in Europe and North America. The Western missionaries who founded many of these churches in the 19th century had a generally negative attitude towards African culture and thought-forms; thus, African converts to Christianity were expected to give up their own cultural ways and to put on Western culture. They were taught a new religious language, new forms of worship, new songs, new doctrines – in short, an entirely new spirituality.

Not all members of the historic churches in Africa today remain entirely submerged in Western culture. A growing number of Christians within these churches are becoming convinced that the insistence that an African must give up his or her own culture and adopt Western culture in order to be a Christian is contrary to the fundamental insight conveyed by the incarnation of Jesus Christ – the Word who became flesh and *lived among us* (cf. John 1:14).

It is especially in worship, healing ceremonies and pastoral counselling that African independent churches express their embrace of African culture. Unlike the historic churches, they use music with an African rhythm and idioms. The language used in worship appeals to the experiences and concerns, the joys and hopes of Africans. G. Chavunduka notes that many members of independent churches also practise some form of traditional medicine and call themselves prophets.

In other words, the cornerstone of the spirituality of these churches is the African worldview, rooted in the daily experiences of life and expressed through the rituals of the community of faith, which serve as a bridge connecting the everyday life of the people with *Mwari*, and thus shaping their lives, sustaining and upholding them. In his book *The Challenge of Africa*, K. Busia describes the important role played by rituals in the Akan culture of Ghana; but what he has to say applies elsewhere in the continent as well:

> Rituals surround seasonal community festivals as well as the critical periods of an individual's life. Planting, harvesting and fishing, birth, puberty, marriage – these are the occasions for the community of the kin-group to come together, to join in song and dance or in ritual to give expression to the sense of the group's solidarity or sense of dependence on the ancestors or other spiritual powers.

Because they have liberated themselves from the Western models, structures and cultural approaches which have consistently condemned African identity, independent churches are growing rapidly. They are able to make their own decisions while the Western-oriented churches must in many cases still refer to their mother churches when they make decisions on such issues as liturgy and doctrine.

It is evident that the Western-oriented churches are often fearful of the power the traditional rites might exercise on African Christians. This came home to me when I took part in a project to adapt and Christianize traditional African rites surrounding birth, marriage and burial. The aim was to offer pastoral help for church members who are practising these rituals outside the Christian context. The response of the majority of church members, both ordained persons and laity, was negative. Obviously, many would prefer to maintain the Western rites, even though these do not express their experiences and will thus inevitably be artificial, rather than risk being confronted by the power of the traditional practices. The result is an ambiguous spirituality. Christian liturgy and traditional rites co-exist, but they have no connection with each other. The inference which many draw is that traditional rites are thus somehow outside the realm of God's creation and therefore evil. But how can we as African Christians in the mainline churches "turn to God", as the WCC assembly theme calls us to do, without involving our total being?

There are signs of hope for the development of an authentic African Christianity. At the time of the Amsterdam assembly, few of those present would have given any thought to the possibility of a distinctive African church music or African spirituality or African theology. Within the relatively short period of 50 years and despite the limited possibilities compared with some other parts of the world, Africa has produced many theologians of stature as well as Christian laypeople who have had a high profile on the international scene and in their own national context in church and world alike. Terms such as "indigenization", "inculturation", "adaptation" and "contextualization" have begun to make an impact in promoting a more African-rooted Christianity, also in the Western-oriented churches. Many African universities and seminaries now offer courses in such disciplines as African theology, African music, African worship, African traditional religion.

The need for an African ecumenism

But if the growth of African Christianity as experienced in the independent churches is to enrich the entire church of God on the continent, the Western-oriented churches must approach these churches positively and be ready to draw some lessons from them. African Christians must work at overcoming the serious rift between the Western-oriented churches and the independent churches. But ecumenical dialogue for Christian unity, it must be acknowledged, has not been a priority among the historic churches in Africa themselves, even when their mother churches in Europe and North America have moved towards increasingly closer relations.

To take one example, the historic *Baptism, Eucharist and Ministry* document from the Faith and Order commission of the World Council of Churches, sent to WCC member churches in 1982 and reflecting years of careful discussion of these theological issues which have so often divided churches, is virtually unknown in Africa. This document and a host of other ongoing ecumenical dialogues have helped member churches of the WCC to discover what other churches actually teach. In the process, they have not only begun to remove some of the barriers that have divided them for centuries but have also come to a deeper understanding of their own teachings. Yet while this is going on, the church in Africa seems for the most part content to sit passively and comfortably on the sidelines, as if the quest for Christian unity were an option rather than a central mandate of the Christian faith.

If the historic churches in Africa were genuinely interested in and concerned about the catholicity or universality of the church, the *Baptism, Eucharist and Ministry* document and other agreed ecumenical statements ought to have found a more substantial resonance. The fact that Africans inherited a divided church from Western missionaries is no excuse for them to remain mere spectators of the ecumenical movement. After all, many Africans living today were born under a colonial or apartheid system; but they did not hesitate to struggle against the political status quo in order to achieve their liberation. Why should they hesitate to join the struggle against the divisions they inherited in their churches?

If African churches wish to give meaning to their own claim that they have "come of age", then they must take seriously their divisions and work much more strenuously to bring about unity. Christians from the West who visit Africa for the first time are often shocked by how pronounced the divisions among local churches in fact are. And the failure of African churches to engage in this dialogue at the local level is reflected in the minimal effect which African input has had on international theological discussions.

The challenge to the church in Africa in the next millennium is to develop a theology which will enable African Christians to *own* the church instead of being mere custodians of it. The ownership of Christianity carries with it a deep sense of accountability, responsibility and commitment. Africans cannot *own* Eurocentric or ethnocentric Christianity unless it is entirely immersed into African spirituality and is born again. That is what "incarnation" is all about. It transforms those who are born again, causing them to grow into the image of Christ.

The call to "Turn to God – Rejoice in Hope" comes precisely as an appeal for such radical transformation in the life of African Christianity. It is an invitation to new life. To be sure, that means letting go of the old life, which can often be a painful and disillusioning process. But there is no transformation and no resurrection without the death of the old.

Many Christians in Africa are yearning to work in the mission of the church alongside like-minded Christians, authentic brothers and sisters who have their own identity. These people are those who know that they are redeemed and who share the story of their salvation. They confess that Jesus Christ is the Lord and saviour who has redeemed them in their own unique situation. Responding to the invitation to "turn to God", they wish to proclaim together the good news of hope and new life in a world gripped by doubt and meaninglessness, a world that is wounded and in despair. It is in such a suffering world, with all its injustices, that we are all called to live out our faith, our mission and our service.

3. Jubilee and African Realities

A Zimbabwean journalist, writing in *The Financial Gazette* of 22 May 1997, expressed in blunt terms what many people around the world would probably consider "the African condition": "As an African... you are forced to regard your very being as a curse. Existing in subhuman bondage, engulfed by hopelessness, disease and destitution, there is often more to mourn about than there is cause for celebration."

The jubilee call to "Turn to God – Rejoice in Hope" is rooted in the conviction that God is not indifferent to this situation. John Pobee has written eloquently of this:

> The Holy Spirit continues to grieve over the destitution and poverty of vast masses of people; over the gap between the luxuriant affluence of the few and the misery of whole populations; over death from starvation; over wars and threats of wars; over terrorism, state-owned and private; over the culture and cult of profit and over economics as if people did not matter; over the prostitution of resources for nuclear weapons, Star Wars and other insanities...; over racist mind-sets and separatist traditions; over the marginalization and multifarious degradation of women in many lands; over the so-called democracies which impose and support dictatorships and thieves who rule by martial law and assassination. God weeps, his Christ sheds tears and his Spirit grieves.

It is under the guidance of the Holy Spirit that Jesus announced his programme for bringing about freedom and joy to the oppressed of his day (Luke 4:18ff.). That was the central message of his mission. Similarly, the central message of the mission of the church today – in Africa as elsewhere – is to proclaim the good news to the poor and disadvantaged of our own societies. This is a message that demands from us a prophetic role as well, calling us as churches to be in the forefront of condemning corruption and abuse of power – including that by our own leaders at every level – and to work towards the establishment of more democratic and accountable societies. Where the church is instead co-opted into a system that denies justice to the poor, the hungry and the needy, it shows that it has turned its back on the gift of the Holy Spirit.

Two things are important to bear in mind as we consider how the call to jubilee comes at an assembly of the World Council of Churches being held on this continent where "there is often more to mourn about than there is cause for celebration". The first is the ecumenical dimension of the call. The churches who will gather in Harare understand themselves as the body of Christ. And the apostle Paul, in his famous explanation of this image of the church as a body, reminds us that "if one member suffers, all suffer together with it; if one member is honoured, all rejoice together with it" (1 Cor. 12:26). The call to jubilee is thus a call to solidarity.

The second thing to remember is that the call to jubilee is not a general call to celebrate as though we could do so apart from the realities of daily life. The appeal to "Turn to God – Rejoice in Hope" comes against the background of very concrete situations; and if the participants gathered in Harare do not speak to these concrete aspects of the human condition, their words will be empty and escapist piety.

What are some of the major realities of life on the African continent today to which the churches gathered at the assembly in Harare will be called to speak a prophetic word of repentance, conversion, joy and hope? As we look briefly at some of these situations which make the Spirit grieve and to which the churches of the world are called to respond in solidarity, we will see, of course, that many of these realities are not only characteristic of Africa.

Uprooted people

Africa hosts more refugees than any other continent. International observers says that there are probably about 5 million people in Africa who have been forced to flee their own countries for a variety of reasons. This figure does not include the men, women and children who have been driven from their homes but remain within the borders of their own country. Often the situation of these internally displaced persons is more precarious than that of refugees, who may receive some international protection – and their numbers are probably even higher. Furthermore, the number of homeless and landless people, many now living on the streets of Africa's large cities, is increasing daily.

The central reality of the life of the refugee is one of powerlessness. Marginalization, victimization and exploitation by institutions or individuals are daily experiences. Many of these millions are separated from loved ones and families, without any assurance of ever being reunited with them. Even those who have received some official status as refugees face a life that is governed and controlled by numerous provisions limiting their freedom of movement and freedom to work. It is a life surrounded by sorrow and despair.

In many cases, the roots of the refugee's plight lie in the corruption and oppression of the political system in his or her country of origin. That was the case with a student at the university who came to me recently for counselling. Listening to his account was a devastating experience for me; yet I realized how many millions of other refugees are not even in a position to articulate their plight:

> When I was a little boy, like any other normal kid, I had lots of dreams of who I would be and what I would do in the future. I was quite certain that I would bring my dreams to reality as I grew up, because I had the talent, potential and determination for achieving them. However, these dreams have not turned out the way I thought. Some unfortunate circumstances stepped in and blocked me from realizing them...

> Living in exile is the strongest personal loss that can be experienced by a human being. At 24 I suddenly find myself on the run, an experience that no one could even prepare for or accept as the characteristic event of one's life. The experience closest to such uprootedness would probably be death...

> Why do we have refugees in Africa? Is it because there are so many dictators around us who go on unchallenged? If so, where is the church? In order to destroy death, God intervened with his son and Jesus commissioned his church to continue the same intervention.

Right now I have no country to live in, yet there are many others in a worse situation than mine. But I hope that one day I will find a place to call a home. I do not want to be a refugee. I have hands and legs, and I do not want to rely on others. Please stop killings, stop wars, stop dictatorships.

"Turn to God – Rejoice in Hope." Perhaps there is no one who has more hope in God than a refugee for whom all human hopes have vanished. This hope is poignantly expressed in the story of a refugee in Burundi, a country which has been bleeding from a violent ethnic conflict for many years. Like thousands of others in the Great Lakes region of central Africa, this man was obliged to leave his home in Bujumbura and run for his life. All he took along for provisions were a torn blanket to cover his body at night and a life-sized wooden cross which he carried under his arm.

What a naive faith! Surely that is how many of us respond when hearing of a person whose most prized possession, the one thing he could not leave behind when fleeing for his life, was a cross. Yet it was this cross which provided inner solace, comfort and security to this man, a hope which no human power could snatch away. Day and night, he walked with this cross, drawing from it the spiritual sustenance and energy to move on. In the loneliness of the tropical forest, this man entered into a new relationship with the Lord, the "I Am" who encountered Moses when he was a refugee in the wilderness, the "I Am" who cannot remain indifferent to the cries of his people suffering under an unjust and oppressive system (Exodus 3).

This God who says "I Am" is not in our comfortable homes, our modern cities, our lovely church buildings. This God is with the men, women and children who are on the run for their lives, those who have no citizenship in the country of their birth, the homeless and the stateless ones. Outside, in the dark where they live, Christ's light shines; in the cold the refugee experiences his warmth. Refugees depend on God for their help because they are outside the walls; and it was outside the walls where their Saviour was crucified (Heb.

13:12), where he was left to meet death alone and lonely and abandoned (cf. Psalm 22).

Everything that matters happens at the centre of the village, at the "commons" or community hall. Outside, there is nothing of importance. It is the place of darkness and chaos, the meeting place of the sick, the vagrant, the homeless, the squatters, the expendables, the voiceless, the disenfranchised, the refugees. They meet there to share their miseries with each other and to share their plight with the one who was crucified. It is outside, where there is no provision for tomorrow, that the disadvantaged of this world, excluded by their fellow humans who have means and resources, depend on God for sustenance, protection and security.

In his own way, the Burundian refugee with a cross under his arm was announcing and inaugurating the year of the Lord's favour. He was also proclaiming God's sovereignty over and God's judgment upon the greedy and oppressive warlords who continue to cause human suffering. For this refugee, the cross was not just a decorative Christian symbol; the Jesus of Nazareth to whom the cross points is someone alive and present and grieving with him.

At the assembly in Harare the cross will be present to remind those attending of the agonies of this world in which God took human form. It will call us to pray that God will enable us to recognize the suffering of our wounded world, and to turn to God with our eyes open to those who are outside our communities, beyond our national boundaries, outside the walls.

Slavery in Africa today

The shameful story of the capture of millions of Africans in the 17th to 19th centuries and of their forced transport, under unimaginably inhumane conditions, to North and South America and the Caribbean, where they were sold into a life of toil as slaves on plantations and in mines, is well known. The consequences of this evil commerce are still felt, not only in the countries to which the slaves were sent but also in Africa, which lost millions of its able-bodied sons and daughters. But many people would probably be astonished to learn that the practice of slavery is still a reality in some parts of Africa to this day. A story in *Time* magazine in July 1996 described a "quick and uncomplicated" transaction in the remote southern Sudanese town of Manyiel: "There was not even any haggling over the price... A trader eagerly accepted a stack of currency worth about US$1000. Moments later he delivered the merchandise – a pair of slaves."

Some months later a story in the Zimbabwean daily *The Herald* described a related kind of transaction in southern Sudan:

> The group of women and children have the eyes of the hunted. They have learned the silence of fear, the knowledge that survival depends on remaining still, small and unnoticed. Some are here under the tree along with others who have scraped together the ransom for them. Others will be freed later.

> The intermediary is gaunt and smiling in his white robe and skull cap, delighted to be freeing slaves. "These people are my brothers." But the altruism vanishes when I enquire about his plans for his share of the money. "I will go with it and eat and drink from it." He grins. Beneath the tree, the 13-year-old Bol Kuol squats down with visible sadness in his eyes.

How do we understand the message of jubilee, the call to "Turn to God – Rejoice in Hope", in the light of the experience of Bol Kuol? Or from the perspective of all those others who are still waiting to be ransomed?

Our inclination is often to follow the advice of a Shona proverb, "*Nhamo yemumwe hairambirwi sadza*" – "Someone else's trouble is no reason to deny yourself food." And so, although we feel a twinge of sorrow when we read stories about the Bol Kuols of this world or see the terrible images of suffering people on our television screens, we do not lose much sleep over it. We tune back to our own relatively peaceful situations. We are concerned, to be sure, but we carry on with our routine, eager to convince ourselves that there is not really much that we can do in the face of these stories of suffering – which are only a small sampling of the worldwide situation of refugees, asylum-seekers, victims of human rights violations, political conflicts and wars.

In the face of this attitude of ours comes the call in Jesus' parable of the judgment, the call to give food to the hungry, drink to those who thirst and clothing to the naked, to welcome the stranger and visit those in prison, for "just as you did it to one of the least of these who are members of my family, you did it to me" (Matt. 25:40). We need not look far in our situations for ways to answer that call. The asylum-seekers among us stand out as strangers. Is the church ready to offer welcome in the form of sanctuary, hospitality and material support? Where there is political conflict, is the church ready to intervene or mediate? Is it ready to engage itself in the cause of freedom for those who are enslaved?

For centuries, the adherents of African traditional religion have sought help in bearing their suffering by turning to traditional healers who try to get to the root causes of their pain, sometimes successfully, sometimes not. For many Christians in Africa, faith in the God who sent his Son to experience human suffering on the cross and thereby to overcome death is their sole comfort, the only assurance that can alleviate their pain. Are the churches in Africa and the churches around the world who will gather in Harare ready to give substance to that faith?

As we celebrate the jubilee assembly, we will have to remind each other about the contexts in which we celebrate it. We will have to recognize that the original proclamation of the jubilee in the Old Testament brought consolation and liberation to those whose weakness in society had made them slaves. For them the theme of jubilee, the message of God's grace and liberation which Jesus later announced in his own preaching, had to do with concrete, practical realities, not just with observing yet another religious festival. So, too, the church is called today to make the jubilee message a concrete, practical reality for the slaves of our contemporary world, to look at their plight as our brothers and sisters, as members of Jesus' family, and to make it our own. At the same time, the jubilee vision must also be proclaimed as good news to the other slaves of our time – those who live in bondage to affluence, racism, nationalism, sexism. All of us are in need of God's grace.

Land and landlessness

Besides its proclamation of freedom to those in bondage, the jubilee message includes another element that is of particular relevance in many African countries, the issue of land.

In the assembly host country of Zimbabwe, land is a particularly controversial question; and in my book *My Right to Land: A Theology of Land in Zimbabwe* I have tried to outline the role that land has played and still plays in the history of our country. Zimbabwe's soil is stained with the blood of the victims of the wars that have been fought here, crying out like the blood of Abel (Gen. 4:10). Among those who survived these wars are today's displaced and landless peasants. Unfortunately, the process of dispossession which was introduced by the colonial settlers did not come to an end when Zimbabwe became independent in 1980. It has continued, with the beneficiaries today being the new black elite who own massive tracts which they do not use while rural peasants have no land on which to sustain themselves. How will Zimbabweans and other Africans who have been dispossessed of ancestral lands understand the biblical jubilee?

The Bible as a whole certainly gives attention to the question of land. Besides the regulations set forth in Leviticus 25 for the jubilee, land is the theme of one of the best-known texts in the Psalms: "The earth is the Lord's and all that is in it" (Psalm 24:1). No human being, it would seem, may claim permanent ownership of land. Jesus' Sermon on the Mount includes the well-known promise to the dispossessed poor, "Blessed are the meek, for they shall inherit the land" (Matt. 5:5). The poor are to receive back the land from which they have been dispossessed because it is their "inheritance" (cf. the story of King Ahab's attempts to steal the vineyard of Naboth recorded in 1 Kings 21:1-16). The prophets' writings regularly denounce land-grabbing; and Micah (2:1-2) pronounces a woe on

> those who devise wickedness
> and evil deeds on their beds!
> When the morning dawns, they perform it,
> because it is in their power.
> *They covet fields and seize them...*

Yet land as a biblical theme has been seriously neglected by the church throughout the centuries. The law of the jubilee as a justice issue is not typically part of the curriculum in theological schools and seminaries. The subject seems to be considered minor and unimportant.

When the missionaries came to Africa to plant the church, they brought with them their European attitudes towards land. In Europe the church owned vast tracts of land, and the church authorities were part of the dominant class which dispossessed the poor peasants. So, too, the missionaries joined with the colonial settlers to grab land from their converts. According to African traditions, this land was considered a gift from God to be shared equally by all members of the community. It was the missionaries and settlers who turned it into private property which could belong in perpetuity to one individual or one family.

At the same time, many missionaries put all the emphasis in their preaching on "righteousness" rather than "justice", thus spiritualizing the message of the gospel. Poverty was proclaimed to Africans as a virtue, even as the missionaries who preached this were accumulating substantial material wealth. While Africans were being pushed off the land, the colonial settlers were busy parcelling out vast tracts to each other, particularly the land whose soil was the most fertile or which had mineral wealth lying beneath it. The communal land ownership system of the Africans was thus completely destroyed and the converts were reduced to the status of impoverished farm labourers. The church of the missionaries did not consider that their proclamation of God's "righteousness" had any implications for this situation; and in the face of the land grabs by which the white settlers consolidated their power they remained passive and indifferent – and indeed sometimes themselves reaped the material benefits.

A rare exception to this was Arthur Shearly Cripps, an Anglican missionary who came to Zimbabwe in 1901 and ended up fighting against the colonial government and his fellow missionaries who were depriving Africans of their land. Cripps wrote in a letter to his brother:

> People talk about the need for medical missionaries, but in a place like southern Africa, what a call for *legal* missionaries there is! If I had my time over and were going to those parts of Africa where the African is up against injustice, I think I would try to qualify in law.

In his way, Cripps had a clearer understanding of the message of jubilee than most of his fellow missionaries.

The biblical mandate to return land to its original owners would come as a welcome call among the landless in Zimbabwe today. But the church, which has not addressed this issue, may have difficulty speaking credibly about it. Moreover, when the jubilee was proclaimed in Old Testament times, it was within the confines of a single nation whose citizens understood themselves as bound by a covenant with the Lord. The provisions of the jubilee were directed at the individual members of that community. Today, the context is different. In many parts of Africa and Asia and Latin America, the most serious forms of land-grabbing are those being practised against indigenous communities by giant agribusinesses and multinational minerals corporations.

Will the jubilee motif of the eighth assembly and the call to turn to God in concrete and specific acts of faithfulness encourage the churches in the powerful countries to exert influence on their governments to counter land speculation and dispossession in the powerless and materially poorer parts of the world? And will the church in the poorer countries be emboldened to preach against the injustices practised by those in power who collaborate with the absentee landlords for their own personal benefit, thus causing political instability, turmoil, poverty and dispossession among many of their own fellow-citizens?

The debt crisis

A major element of the biblical jubilee was the forgiveness of debts. In the agrarian society of ancient Israel, the burden of debt was often linked with the problem of landlessness, as poor farmers unable to repay borrowed money were forced to turn over their land to their creditors and were thus pushed further to the margins economically. The jubilee legislation provided for the return of land lost in this way to the families to whom it had originally belonged. Echoes of this jubilee theme can be found in the Lord's prayer, in which Jesus links the forgiveness of our own debts with our willingness to forgive those who are indebted to us. While many recent translations of this best known of Christian prayers have tended to spiritualize this petition by translating the Greek word for "debts" as "trespasses" or "sins", the fact remains that the Lord's prayer is a jubilee prayer even if we may try to avoid its more concrete implications.

The "debt crisis" in the world today, touching particularly the South, including many African countries, has different origins and a different nature from the situation of landless peasants in Israel. But the consequences it has for millions of people in these countries mean that the churches attending a jubilee assembly of the World Council of Churches are obliged to consider the implications of this biblical theme for the contemporary situation.

What does the debt crisis mean for African countries? President Benjamin Mkapa of Tanzania, welcoming the World Council of Churches' Faith and Order commission at its plenary meeting in Moshi, Tanzania, in August 1996, put it this way (an extended excerpt from his address was published in *The Ecumenical Review*, Oct. 1996, pp.520-24):

> One of the problems that act as a millstone around the neck of Africa is the unbearable debt burden. External debt for sub-Saharan Africa rose from US$84.3 billion in 1980 to a staggering projection of $313 billion in 1994. Tanzania, for example, has an external debt of $7 billion. If we were to apportion this debt to every man, woman and child, each one of them would be indebted to the magnitude of their total earnings for two-and-

a-half years. And if we were to spend all our national foreign exchange earnings to pay off this debt it would still take us over 12 years to do so.

Eventually, we have to ask, shall we let our children die of curable or preventable diseases, prevent them from going to school, let people drink polluted water – just to pay off this debt? For this is indeed what is happening. We in Tanzania now spend about 30 percent of our budget to service only a part of our debt obligations. In the 1995-96 financial year, to service our national debt we spent an amount sufficient to meet the budgeted expenditures of seven major government ministries: home affairs, defence, agriculture, education, health, finance and science and technology...

There is a perception that all Africa wants is aid and, as long as aid is forthcoming, there is no need to give Africa further attention. This is wrong. Our relationship must be based on much more than aid... Africa needs genuine and all-round friendship, partnership and cooperation with Europe and other developed countries. We need each other...

Concluding his remarks, Mkapa linked the search for Christian unity, the priority of the Faith and Order commission, with the search for the unity of humankind as a whole:

We are all God's children, and as such we need to work for unity in our diversity. The humanity of each society is measured by the way it treats its more vulnerable members. On the international plane, the humanity of a nation should be measured according to the attention it pays to Africa and the other least developed countries.

The debt crisis in the South is a creation of the North, which has distorted the concept of a free market in the world. All human communities have always had a market, whether in a house or in an open space in the community. In villages all around Africa, as elsewhere in the South, the marketplace serves as a meeting point where villagers come not only to exchange merchandise but also to share ideas and information, the everyday links that build human community. At the Harare assembly, this reality of African society will be

32

reflected in the *Padare*, the Shona word for marketplace, where churches, councils of churches and other ecumenical partners of the WCC will have a place to share with delegates information about and insights gained from their own ministry.

But the "free market" as it operates in the world today is something quite different from this traditional expression of human community. The difference was trenchantly explained by one of the study groups at the 1996 conference of the International Association of Mission Studies (whose theme was "God and Mammon: Economics and Conflict") in their report on "The Powers of the Market and the Power of God":

> Today we are faced with a new kind of market, determined by the ideology of neo-colonialism and new conservatism, which is global, unstable and unfair. Those with bargaining power, usually the economic powers of the North but also allied interests in the third world, impose their will for their own gain on those with less or no bargaining power, usually in the third world, but also the poor in the North. This market is therefore not a *free* place nor an even playing field. Transnational companies make state control and regulation difficult or impossible.

> The myth of the impersonal market power needs to be exposed. The market is basically relationships between people where economic structures may be used by some to exploit and oppress others for personal or corporate gain of money and power. Even countries which have developed a form of market economy which has room for progressive social politics are being forced by the global market economy to go back on some of them...

> The continent which according to statistical estimates will be the most Christian by the year 2000, Africa, is also the poorest, contributing only 2 percent to world trade.

Political ideologies and economic powers are now the new major players in the marketplace. The collaboration between the minority rich in the North and the self-aggrandized minority in the South makes the marketplace a battlefield where the poor majority in the South – and the growing minority of poor in the North – suffer at the hands of the rich and powerful.

The eighth assembly takes place at a time when 20 percent of the world's population controls 84 percent of the world's resources – and the gap is growing. It takes place in a world where 40,000 people, most of them children, die every day of starvation and of preventable diseases. The economies of the two-thirds world are controlled by international financial institutions such as the World Bank, the International Monetary Fund (IMF) and the World Trade Organization (WTO, formerly GATT). These institutions are in effect modern slave-masters.

The biblical jubilee cannot be separated from questions about appropriation and expropriation of resources. An ecumenical celebration under the theme of jubilee must be a moment of truth, when we put in order our relationship with each other and with God. It is a time to discover our identity as a redeemed people of God, a time to renew our faithfulness to the gospel, a time of reconciliation and of commitment to issues of peace and justice – including the issue of the unjust external debt which is threatening the peace and stability of so many countries today. Jubilee is a time of compassion, a time to create a more humane society and to respect God's creation. The jubilee can help us to move towards the future with a sense of renewal and rededication to our common humanity in appreciation of the resources God has given us. In Africa, however, it is impossible to talk about such a jubilee without thinking in terms of the cancellation of debt. People in Africa and throughout the South must be relieved from their debt-slavery. Only then can we respond to the sound of the drumbeat of life.

The assembly will be a meeting point for Christians from both creditor and debtor countries. Together, they must say No to a market whose effect is the exploitation of the poor. The debt crisis should not be viewed as a purely economic issue, but as an issue which tests the credibility of our faith in God the creator, who wills justice among his children. Our response as Christians to the evil that dominates the market-place is to call all people to turn to God.

The AIDS pandemic

We cannot conclude this brief survey of the challenges facing Africa which set the context for the jubilee assembly without mentioning a serious tragedy whose origins are rela-tively recent but whose dimensions become more apparent with each passing year: the HIV/AIDS pandemic. The global reach of this epidemic and its serious consequences – for individuals, for families and also for societies – is well-known; and the central committee of the World Council of Churches, meeting in Johannesburg in 1994, called for the formation of a high-level consultative group to study all the dimensions of HIV/AIDS and their implications for the church. Its report (published as *Facing AIDS: The Challenge, The Churches' Response*, WCC Publications, 1997) notes that

> for many of us HIV/AIDS has acted as a spotlight, exposing and revealing many iniquitous conditions in our personal and com-munity lives which until now we have not been willing to con-front... It exposes any silence and indifference of the churches, challenging them to be better informed, more active and more faithful witnesses to the gospel of reconciliation in their own lives and in their communities.

> Increasing numbers of people worldwide are falling sick, suf-fering physically, emotionally and spiritually – many in aban-donment and desolation... The effects of HIV/AIDS are impov-erishing people, breaking their hearts, violating their human rights and wreaking havoc on their bodies and spirits.

Over the past decade or so, AIDS has claimed a frightful number of lives in sub-Saharan Africa. At the time of this writing, some 16 million of the world's 24.1 million reported cases are found in this region, many in the age group from 25 to 45. A growing number of HIV-positive mothers die soon after the delivery of their babies, who themselves have a very limited chance of survival beyond the age of five. As a result, more and more children become orphans, posing another challenge to already fragile societies, as extended families can no longer cope with the enormous burden of looking after the children of deceased relatives.

An African story told by M.C. Mukoyogo and G. Williams (in *AIDS Orphans: Strategies for Hope*, 1991) puts personal faces to the statistics:

> Nine-year-old Lenina often sits on her own in the yard, a distant look on her face. Whenever this happens, her grandmother knows she is thinking about her dead parents, and tries to distract her with conversation or by asking her to help with a job in the kitchen. Lenina's father died of AIDS four months ago, her mother three weeks later...

> Seventy-two-year-old Mulungi is now the family's main breadwinner. Her husband Kato, who says he was born in 1900, is no longer strong enough to work. The family is just managing to survive on a diet of maize, cassava, sweet potatoes and bananas, with occasional treats of rice, fish and beans. Lenina still attends primary school, but she will have to drop out soon because her grandparents cannot afford to buy her a new uniform and pay the school fees and other expenses. The children often talk about their parents. Sometimes when Mulungi gives them maize porridge without sugar (because she cannot afford to buy any), one of the young children will say, "Grandmother, when our mother was alive she would give us porridge with lots of sugar."

On society as a whole the AIDS pandemic has adverse economic effects, for the early death of the most productive members of the society deprives the community of vital human resources. And there is no cure in sight to stop this epidemic.

Especially tragic is the way in which children in Africa – as elsewhere in the world – are being caught up in the AIDS epidemic, just as they are caught up in violent conflicts and wars, subjected to hunger and preventable diseases, and exploited as discardable sexual commodities or cheap labour. The suffering of children reminds us that we have lost a sense of the sanctity of life.

The jubilee call which Jesus used as the theme of his opening sermon in Nazareth is also a promise of healing. Luke 4:18 speaks specifically of the recovery of sight for the blind; and throughout the four gospels are stories of Jesus' direct intervention in the life of sick and suffering individuals through healing miracles. Thus the jubilee assembly is also a reminder of the call to the churches, in Africa and elsewhere, to be genuinely healing communities, committed to the restoration of health and wholeness and to the eradication of the conditions which threaten and destroy it.

In the face of this, silence is no option. The sacredness of life compels Christians to be the voice of conscience, speaking out for the protection of life against all those who abuse it.

A kairos moment

The image of the "year of the Lord's favour" speaks of a special kind of time, a moment of particular challenge and opportunity expressed in the Greek word *kairos*.

In Africa today, many have the sense of living at such a *kairos* moment. The Zimbabwean journalist whose sombre words about "the African condition" I quoted at the beginning of this chapter went on to describe how listening to an address by South African President Nelson Mandela to the Zimbabwean parliament stimulated his own sense of living in a special time:

> I felt a sudden burst of hope and inspiration. The legendary freedom fighter spoke about the African renaissance, a new dawn or a new chapter, where Africans are at last beginning to direct the course of their destiny.

> In the global arena, Mandela says, "it is a renaissance that must mean that Africa refuses to be a passive onlooker in a changing world, a hapless victim to modern machinations of the forces historically responsible for her woes"... For the ordinary citizen, the African renaissance is a reawakening of the giant from the deep slumber of official corruption, criminal neglect of social responsibility and misrule by African rulers...

37

Only yesterday it was South Africa, then came Zambia and Malawi. Today it's Zaire, now the Democratic Republic of Congo, and tomorrow it will have to be another dictatorship coming to terms with reality. The circus is on the move. So... when some of us decry corrupt and nepotistic tendencies in the leadership and denounce the rape and plunder of national resources by a chosen few, it is not out of a sour grapes mentality or out of misguided cynicism. It is because we see and read the writing on the wall...

It is not easy to be in the same room with Mandela and not be thoroughly inspired to seek change. I was particularly touched by his reference to the swearing-in ceremonies of the leaders of the great kingdoms of Mapungubwe, Great Zimbabwe and Khami, where the presiding officers always reminded the new rulers of their social responsibilities by proclaiming: "You are the chief of everyone, father of orphans and those who suffer."

The biblical *kairos* is of course more than a matter of human social and political changes. The proclamation of jubilee as a *kairos* moment, a time of grace, is linked with the more familiar Old Testament institutions of the sabbatical year (cf. Ex. 23:10ff.) and the weekly sabbath as a day of rest.

Many African communities also observe a periodic day of rest. For example, the Shona people of Zimbabwe, who are agriculturalists by tradition, have a regular day of rest known as *chisi*. For the rural peasant farmers, *chisi* was not just a day of freedom from labour, but a day of celebrating life in community, a sacred day; thus working on this day was an act of disobedience against the community and its religious norms.

Jesus proclaimed the sabbath as a day not of idleness and boredom, but of sharing God's time by healing and helping and consoling and comforting one another. Understood as a time for freeing people from pain and hunger, oppression and diseases, a sabbath and a jubilee which affirm life and healing are rooted in the recognition of time as God's gift to us – contrary to our usual inclination to feel good about spending a few hours helping someone else as though it were *our* time we were giving to the needy. Time is not something mysterious or detached from us like a commodity. It is part of us and in us and around us. Every minute, hour, day, month, year is given to us; and our response is to make it holy time by sharing it with one another.

Coming on the occasion of the WCC's fiftieth anniversary and a year before the turn of the century and millennium, the eighth assembly can be a *kairos* moment for the churches of the world. But it will only prove to be such a time if the churches are ready to hear the full implications of the call to "Turn to God – Rejoice in Hope".

4. The Ecumenical Future and the Churches of Africa

The Harare assembly will not only be an occasion for celebrating the signs of ecumenical progress over the past 50 years, and for listening to testimonies of life and faith from churches around the world. More importantly, it will be a moment to look ahead to the ecumenical future. Participants will share not only their stories but also their visions and dreams about how to realize the goal of visible church unity, deepen their collaboration and solidarity with each other and overcome the polarization and marginalization that still plague their fellowship.

The unity of the church

The founding of the WCC in Amsterdam was the fruit of a growing awareness of the unity of the church as something willed by its Lord. On the night before his death, Jesus prayed to his Father for the unity of his disciples and for those who were to follow them: "that they may be one, as we are one" (John 17:11). Besides giving the *basis* of the unity sought by the ecumenical movement – the oneness of the holy Trinity – this prayer goes on to give the *purpose* of that search for unity: "so that the world may believe that you have sent me" (v.21). The ecumenical movement thus participates in the commission Jesus gave his disciples before leaving them: "As the Father has sent me, so I send you" (John 20:21).

In a world increasingly divided along political, economic, religious and racial lines, a church which is growing together in unity helps to commend the Christian gospel, while continuing Christian disunity is a counter-witness to the church's own proclamation. The fact that the goal of unity which animated those who were present at the Amsterdam assembly in 1948 has not yet been attained suggests that the church has not yet fully grasped the message it has to proclaim to the world.

Theological dialogues among divided churches, including the many bilateral conversations which have flourished since the entry of the Roman Catholic Church into the ecumenical movement with the Second Vatican Council more than 30 years ago, have registered many small steps moving the churches towards a greater understanding of each other. This in itself is a cause for celebration; but it certainly does not warrant remaining complacent about the status quo, for much remains to be done before the mission is accomplished. These dialogues, both those among WCC member churches and those involving the Roman Catholic Church and other non-member churches, must be intensified as the church moves into the third millennium.

The purpose of calling the churches to the unity which they confess God has given them belongs to the whole work of the WCC, undergirding all of its initiatives in mission, justice, service and education. The quest for visible church unity has been a particular priority of the Faith and Order commission. Through its numerous studies bringing together theologians and church leaders from around the world and from all Christian confessions (including some not represented in the WCC), but perhaps most of all through the publication of its landmark text on *Baptism, Eucharist and Ministry* (1982), the work of this commission has advanced the cause of church unity in many ways. As it looks ahead to the third millennium, it would seem that Faith and Order should intensify its attention to the actual issues of faith and order arising in the churches of the South, which were not represented in Amsterdam in 1948, much less in Lausanne in 1927 when the Faith and Order commission was established.

As we search in our divided world for the oneness not only of the church but of all of humanity, we hear voices asking probing questions about the nature of unity:
– How can we be one with those who oppress us?
– How can we be one with those who dispossess us?
– How can we be one with those who exploit us?
– How can we be one with those who dehumanize us?
– How can we be one with those who discriminate against us because of our gender?
– How can we be one with those who marginalize us?

At the same time we hear other voices asking different kinds of questions, just as difficult, about unity:

- How can we be one with beggars and street people?
- How can we be one with those of other races?
- How can we be one with Muslims or Hindus?
- How can we be one with those whose views and practices regarding human sexuality differ from our own?
- How can we be one with criminals?

Christians should be in the vanguard of those working for the kind of human unity in which all may live together in harmony and peace as God has intended. But if it is to be credible, that search for unity must begin with the churches themselves. In a spirit of repentance, we must regain a sense of the scandal of our divisions, a feeling of dissatisfaction with and embarrassment over the slowness of our own paths towards unity. We need to be reminded that the church is God's and exists for God. Where the church is at work, God is present, leading it into truth, shaping and transforming it. In this vein we are called to turn to God, to rediscover the truth and will of God under the guidance of the Holy Spirit. The God who has promised, "I am with you always, to the end of the age" (Matt. 28:20), is the church's primary missionary leading it to unity. The unity of the church and of humankind is Jesus' agenda; it must therefore be ours as well. As African theologian John Pobee has written,

> Ministry must be God-centred; for we go out as ambassadors of the Creator God, King of kings, Lord of lords, the Almighty... Mission is not my agenda or crusade, it is God's agenda, which must be discerned also in the world around us.

To fulfill its mission, the ecumenical movement will have to continue to engage its members in serious dialogue about church unity. It will have to continue to share a common recognition of the dignity of all human beings. It will have to continue its involvement in world events as a response to its true calling to bear witness so that the world may come to know God and live together in unity of purpose. "How very good and pleasant it is when kindred live together in unity!" (Ps. 133:1). Where the human family lives together in unity and peace, they also respond together to the drumbeat of life and dance together in harmony.

Sharing of resources

As we move into the third millennium, the acid test for the ecumenical movement will lie in how well it can foster the sharing of resources, both human and material.

Over the fifty years since the Amsterdam assembly, as we noted earlier, there has been a shift in the "centre of gravity" of world Christianity; and this has clear implications for our understanding and practice of ecumenical sharing. In the early years of the ecumenical movement and at the time the WCC was founded, both the quest for unity and the missionary work of the church were almost exclusively in the hands of the churches of the North. The missionary sending agencies provided all the resources – and for a long time all the personnel – and the South was a mere recipient.

Today the churches of the South represent themselves in the WCC. This direct representation in the WCC, along with the dynamic growth of Christianity in many parts of the South, places a profound responsibility on these churches. How do they make their voices heard when questions are asked such as "Who are we?", "What is the mission of the church today and tomorrow?", "What can we do together to achieve our goal of bringing all humanity together under the lordship of Jesus Christ?"

The jubilee of the WCC is a call to continue to proclaim the good news of divine salvation in a world torn apart by wars and conflicts, social and economic injustice and poverty. Jesus' missionary programme as set out in Luke 4 is to continue. But if the ecumenical movement is to encourage and assist this mission of proclaiming love and peace, freedom and justice, repentance and reconciliation, it must allow itself to be led by the power of the Holy Spirit. This proclamation is just as challenging today as it was in Jesus' time and as it was 50 years ago. But the world of 1998 is more complex than the world of 1948. For example, if we speak in terms of "unreached people", it would appear, judging from empty church buildings, that the number of them has greatly increased in the North. In the South, the unreached people are found among adherents of other world religions and traditional religions, who may be not at all impressed by the way Christians have treated each other in the former Yugoslavia or in Rwanda – to take only two recent examples.

The gospel of Christ is about the extension of God's rule to all creatures, reconciling people with God and with each other and with the rest of creation. The gospel has to do with the transformation of all areas of human existence. For African traditional religious thought, the idea of separating the human being into soul and body is unknown. For this reason there is no hierarchy of importance regarding meeting physical needs and meeting spiritual needs. If the gospel is to speak in Africa, it must speak to both kinds of needs.

The first priority in the mission of the church is to enable Christians to understand that those in Christ are new human beings. Theirs is to love and care, not to destroy life; to share resources, not to deny them to others; to forgive, not to hold grudges; to be reconciled, not to rebel; to seek peace and justice for all. The future mission of the ecumenical movement depends on how those "who announce peace, who bring good news, who announce salvation, who say to Zion Your God reigns'" (Isa. 52:7) can give credibility to their message by respecting and encouraging one another and demonstrating their sharing and solidarity on national and international issues of common concern.

Human resources

Despite the limitations imposed by material poverty, political instability, persecution and marginalization, the church in the South is growing quickly; and it is growing without the kind of traditional missionary structures that were developed in the 19th century. Missionary activity is seen as the responsibility of every Christian and it is spontaneous. Many Christians in the South bear witness to the story of Jesus wherever they are without feeling embarrassed to

affirm their faith, whereas in the North most Christians seem
to regard faith as a private matter of personal commitment.

How can the ecumenical movement of the future recognize and then build on these resources found among the
member churches of the WCC in the South? Is the church in
the North ready to recognize itself as living in a missionary
situation? My own experience of several years serving a Ger-
man congregation suggests that Christians in the North, even
those actively engaged in the international ecumenical movement, can be very reluctant to acknowledge the possibility
of missionaries from the South coming to them. This is not,
of course, to say that the churches in Africa should export all
of their missionaries and evangelists, as though there were no
need to nurture the faith of the growing number of Christians
living in the very diverse contexts of Africa itself.

What must happen in world mission is a breakdown of
the distinction between "sending" and "receiving" churches.
All Christians, whether in the North or the South, are com-
missioned to participate in God's mission. "Turn to God –
Rejoice in Hope" is an invitation that comes to all to enter
into a right relationship with each other and with God.

The mission of the church today and in the future is to call
people to become one forgiven and reconciled jubilee community, in which all members are equal partners, a community without majority and minority, a community of commis-
sioned ambassadors of God, called to proclaim the gospel to
all nations. While the ecumenical community may reflect
that diversity in its composition, much remains to be done in
order to change attitudes and make that one diverse community of ambassadors for Christ a reality.

Money

For many years, the very term "resources" in ecumenical
language tended to be a polite synonym for money. Especially through discussions stimulated by the WCC after its
fifth assembly in Nairobi, when some church leaders from
Africa and elsewhere in the South urged a "moratorium" on
sending missionaries and money to their part of the world –

precisely in order to strengthen their mission – the ecumenical understanding of sharing has broadened to include human and spiritual resources. Yet money undeniably continues to play an important role in our relationships as churches.

The members of the missionary movement of the early church began with a vision of entirely sharing material resources with one another: "the whole group of those who believed were of one heart and soul, and no one claimed private ownership of any possessions, but everything they owned was held in common" (Acts 4:32; though Acts 5:1-11 makes clear that not everyone subscribed to this).

As partners in the North know well, the South is a zone of material poverty. Its financial resources are limited and in some cases virtually nonexistent. In southern Africa, for example, the entire economy of a country may depend on having a good rainy season. Yet this material poverty has not prevented the churches in the South from growing. This is an encouragement for the mission of the ecumenical movement. At the same time, many churches in the South suffer from a culture of dependency which has set in over many years, a habit of being on the receiving end of financial support from the North. If the churches in the South have come of age in the ecumenical movement, it is time for them to grapple with the questions of resource-sharing. The claim to have come of age is legitimate, and Africans need not apologize for making it, provided that they recover the sense of self-esteem they lost during the period of colonialism and missionary paternalism. For this to happen they will have to assume full responsibility for the mission and the programme of their churches. They will have to rediscover the needy in their own communities. They will have to become self-reliant and stop depending on handouts from outside. The freedom from slavery announced in the biblical jubilee meant that those who had been dependent on their masters now had to become self-reliant. The jubilee assembly in Harare will have no meaning if African churches choose to continue their old ways of dependency.

If the ecumenical movement is to perform its mission effectively in the 21st century, it will have to learn to distinguish between independence and interdependence, between self-reliance and self-centredness. It will need to draw the lessons from the experience of its younger and more vibrant churches in the South. The gifts God has given to the church are to be used for the common good. Sharing of resources, including financial resources, is thus not an optional extra but an imperative component of the ecumenical vision.

African gifts to the ecumenical movement

Beyond the sharing of human and material resources, the ecumenical movement is also a place for churches from widely diverse contexts to share their distinctive spiritual gifts with each other. In the final section of this chapter, I will suggest three particular gifts which the African churches have to share with the ecumenical movement. The assembly in Harare can be an important occasion for highlighting these contributions.

Community

In African culture, community is the cornerstone for the individual and for his or her survival. Indeed, the individual has no meaning outside the context of the community. The community defines how the individual functions; in turn, the behaviour of the individual affects all the other members of the community. The community is a unit and acts as one. It celebrates life together. At religious festivals, weddings and other social events, its members dance together. At funerals and other tragic moments its members mourn together.

Life is something shared, which is given to the community by God, who is the ultimate link and destiny of the community. Thus young and old, rich and poor act together for the benefit of each person and for the common welfare of the community. This oneness of the community is not limited to its living members, but extends to the "timeless living", who share in the community's joys and sorrows.

A Shona proverb says *"Kandiro kanoenda kunobva kamwe"* – "a good turn deserves another". A person who receives a gift is expected sooner or later to reciprocate. A prosperous individual who turns a deaf ear to the needy of the community will later, in his or her own time of need, find no cooperation when going to the neighbour for a favour. In some instances, such individualists have even been left to bury their own dead without the support of the community – a major task in a rural community where there are no undertakers!

The African concept of community has close parallels with the biblical idea of a community bound together through a covenant which governs it and lays out the boundaries to be observed by its members. The biblical community confesses that Jesus is Lord and that God is a God of justice, so that every member of the community is to practise justice towards every other member for the common welfare. Dispossession, selfishness, and oppression or exploitation of one member by another are contrary to the spirit of the covenant and destroy the unity and life of the community. The biblical idea of community places a high value on inter-human relations; similarly, an African will strive to maintain good relations with the community in order to live long.

Community-building in the ecumenical movement is essential for its survival. African Christians inherited a divided church from the West. At one level, the divisions in African churches today, after a generation of African leadership, are more pronounced than in the mother churches in Europe and North America. Members of an African family who belong to different denominations feel the pain of that reality when they go their separate ways on Sunday morning. They sometimes avoid speaking about their Christian experience because of the differences which this creates.

Yet these divisions do not touch the roots of the traditional life of the African community. They are ignored when the community gathers for weddings or funerals. It is very common in Zimbabwe, for example, to see members of denominations which would otherwise be separated at the

Lord's table partaking of communion together during a requiem mass. In the community's act of farewell to one of its beloved members, denominational barriers fall for a moment. The church leaders, who do not otherwise address the issue of church unity, are powerless to enforce denominational norms in such situations, recognizing the importance people attach to their community. From the African perspective, one might say, there is an unofficial unity-in-existence built on the traditional concept and practice of community. This reality, which has resisted the divisiveness exported from Europe into the body of Christ in Africa, may have something to offer the churches in the ecumenical movement.

Our world is a divided one, and the task of the ecumenical movement from the outset has been to try to build bridges across these divisions. The stumbling blocks on the road to unity cannot be removed by individuals, but only by those committed to building a community of communities. The African entry-point on the road towards church unity is thus a communal approach.

Theological perspectives

A second ecumenical contribution which the church in Africa could offer would be to articulate more clearly its own understandings of the central Christian theological themes of creation and incarnation. What does it mean when Christians say that "the Word became flesh and lived among us" (John 1:14)? According to the gospels, the Word became incarnate in the womb of a Jewish peasant woman from a poor and humble background, living in Palestine when Augustus was the Roman emperor; and she represented all of humanity. When the missionaries, who were of course products of their own time and their own cultures, came to Africa, they proclaimed a gospel enshrined and confined in the culture from which they came – which was not of course the culture in which the Word was incarnated. They failed to see that the incarnation speaks of God's presence in *every* human culture. African Christians in turn need to draw on their own stories and idioms and proverbs in articulating a theology of incarnation that is born from their own worldview. This understanding must then be brought to the ecumenical community, not in order to suggest that it should be enshrined as a universal replacement for the understanding of incarnation imposed by European theology, but as a gift to enrich the understanding of the whole community of the central Christian mystery of God's becoming flesh and living among us.

African oral tradition is very explicit about the idea of God as the Creator who encompasses the land. God is everywhere, embracing the creation; his girdle has no beginning and no end. Because Africans have respect for all of God's creation, their traditional religious beliefs are sometimes referred to as "animistic" or even "primitive". The land is understood as belonging to God. God has given it to humankind. It is thus not to be owned by any individual at the expense of other members of the community. The land is our mother, to be respected, loved and looked after, so that succeeding generations may also benefit from it. Trees and rivers enjoyed the same respect before the Western concept of nature was imposed on Africa and the land and its resources began to be plundered and exploited in the name of "development".

The theology of the environment which more and more Western Christians are beginning to expound has its roots in these so-called "primitive" non-Western cultures, including those of Africa, where nature has traditionally been conceived as sacred, an inseparable part of human existence whose unrestrained exploitation amounts to self-destruction.

Liturgical expression

In worship the gathered community of faith structures its expressions of joy, grief and praise, acknowledging its dependence on God's grace and forgiveness. When a ritual is performed, the community is given time and space to meet God at a deep and precious moment of its life. Religious experience, whether expressed through liturgy or elsewhere, contains an element of renewal. Experience is the key to renewal; without it, the community and the individual cannot turn to God. It is through experience that one reacts or responds to God, like Thomas confronted with the risen Lord (John 20) or Paul on the road to Damascus (Acts 9). Liturgy in the African context will therefore be relevant only when it expresses the experience of African people. Yet the historic churches in Africa have tended to use forms of liturgy produced in Europe and North America and thus lacking the vitality of African spirituality.

African culture, however, is full of ritual expressions which could enrich worship at ecumenical gatherings like the eighth assembly. Already in recent years more and more African music has been introduced into churches elsewhere in the world. Through ecumenical gatherings and in the ongoing exchange of worship resources through the WCC, such songs as the Zimbabwean "Hallelujah" and the South African hymn "Thuma Mina" ("Send me, Lord") have become increasingly familiar to Christians worldwide. And there are many other ritual expressions from African culture which could further enrich ecumenical worship.

While the Western-oriented churches in Africa have tended to retain the static and lifeless forms of worship inherited from the missionaries in the 19th century, which have little to do with local experiences and idioms (and whose use is in fact declining in their countries of origin), the African independent churches offer lively ritual expressions based on local culture. Everyone brings his or her own instrument – drums, *hoshos* (shakes), horns, whistles. There are no professionals set apart to perform; in this dance of life everyone participates. African cultural dances and drama are expressive and full of colour. When Africans dance, they express the joy of life in community, social solidarity, renewal and building of relationships, thus proclaiming their oneness. These are some of the elements which could contribute to the ecumenical movement on the way to the visible unity of the community of Christ worldwide.

"Turn to God – Rejoice in Hope" is a liturgical call to which we can best respond through a lively liturgy expressing our experience as a people of God who are constantly being energized by the spirit of jubilee, a spirit of renewal and transformation. In liturgy we gather together as a community of promise awaiting better things to come. That is our hope. Through worship, this hope links us with each other and with God, giving us confidence in the future which is in God's hands.

Our worship as a people of promise expresses our deep adoration of God our Creator and Redeemer, and our thanksgiving for God's faithfulness to us. We confess our weakness and our failures to trust in God in moments of crisis; and we intercede for the world that disregards the Creator and sustainer of all that is.

The dance of life and the drumbeat of hope

The African dance of life is a liberating and healing experience. Thus Christian liturgy is not only the proclamation of good news to the unreached and unrepentant. It is also the offer of forgiveness and healing to members of the community who through God's grace are renewed and energized to live a new life.

At the Harare assembly, therefore, we will not only look back on our common history of fifty years. We shall also survey new possibilities along the road that leads to the goal of visible unity. In the theme "Turn to God – Rejoice in Hope" we reaffirm our original vision. As a worldwide community each of us will, like the participants in an African dance of life, bring our own uniqueness, to be enjoyed and shared by all, thus making visible our commitment to the principle of unity in diversity.

In an African village, the drumbeat, *Pangu-Pangu-Pangu*, is heard by those far and near, young and old, rich and poor. Members of the community respond to this sound by gathering at the designated place in the village centre in anticipation of taking part in the dance of life. The *Pangu-Pangu-Pangu* of the WCC's eighth assembly is directed to a global village, gathering to meet in Harare. Each participant, old or young, woman or man, black or white, rich or poor, is invited to come fully prepared to dance the dance of life.

To this dance of life each participant will come with a story to tell, and in the preceding chapters I have tried to suggest, from the point of view of an African Christian, some of the concerns which will be on their lips. To be sure, as J.S. Hopewell reminds us in the book *Congregations: Stories and Structures*, "there is always the danger of distortion in relating stories about one's own church – of accentuating the achievements and minimizing the failures". What I have said here indicates my own way of sharing as an African the story of the mission and vocation of the ecumenical movement and the WCC in the past and its hopes for the future. I have tried to avoid the dangers of distortion, of pretending that all is well or lamenting that nothing is well.

But "Turn to God – Rejoice in Hope" is also an invitation to tell a corporate story about the ecumenical movement – where it is coming from and how it has made an impact (or failed to make an impact) on our worldviews and our spiritualities. It is a call to define our corporate identity in a way that takes seriously the many personal stories told by individuals from countless communities, for it is only through what they do and what they contribute to the dance of life that the assembly can be complete.

"Turn to God – Rejoice in Hope" is also a call to the renewal of the ecumenical vision. As a community of faith, we turn to a God who is always present, renewing and transforming the church. Ultimately, the ecumenical movement depends on the power of the Holy Spirit for this renewal. Only through the Holy Spirit can the member churches of the World Council of Churches be empowered to confront the issues, great and small, which threaten to undermine the sacredness of life. At the eighth assembly, daily services, individual meditation, prayers and vigils, plenary and group sessions should work together to give participants that feeling of connectedness without which the dance will lose its rhythm. To drift together towards unity, to dance together the dance of life, is possible only if Christians begin to see the presence of God in the person next to them.